MODERN
WOODBURNING

LEISURE ARTS, INC. • Maumelle, Arkansas

CONTENTS

Welcome 4

Meet Dana 6

Woodburning Basics & Techniques 9

Basic Linework & Filled Areas 18
      Pineapple Cutting Board

Basic Lettering 22
      Family Name Sign

Adding Color 26
      Butterfly Jewelry Hanger

Natural Inspiration 30
      Mountains Ornament

Achieving Fine Details 34
      Gather Serving Tray

Rounded Surfaces 38
      Spoons

Smaller Lettering 42
      Planter Set

Using Multiple Points 46
      Succulent Coasters

Shading 50
      Mandala Wall Hanging

Patterns 54

WELCOME!

Pyrography, or the art of woodburning, has been around since the dawn of history. Originally called pokerwork, the word pyrography translates from Greek to "writing with fire." This art form has come an incredibly long way. Historians suggest the first form of pyrography used charred remains of a fire to create art. This centuries' old craft is making a fresh, fun comeback in the crafting world. Don't feel intimidated—you don't need to be an expert artist or possess expensive equipment to begin woodburning. The accessibility and affordability of modern-day tools allow this hobby to be enjoyed by all!

I am often asked how I got into woodburning. I've always considered myself an artist and craved a creative outlet. I spent years creating pen and ink drawings, as well as watercolor and acrylic paintings. One day while browsing at a craft store, I came across a woodburning tool and bought it on a whim. I can still clearly remember the first time I tried woodburning. Two natural elements, wood and fire, combined to make this remarkably unique art form, and I was immediately in love. There's something so special to me about creating art on real wood slices, the smell of burning wood and the endless canvases available to work on. I love that wood-burned art can add a touch of nature to any living space, bringing the outdoors in.

Modern Woodburning contains everything you need to know to begin the craft, along with my best tips and advice from years of experience. The possibilities are absolutely endless—create beautiful wall art for your home or personalized gifts your loved ones will enjoy for years to come. I hope to inspire you to try woodburning, develop your skills, and discover your own unique style. Fall in love with woodburning with me!

ALL ABOUT DANA

Dana Hoover is a self-taught woodburning artist born and raised in Northeast Ohio. Since childhood, she has felt the constant desire to create and took every high school art class she was able to, falling in love with many different mediums along the way. Dana's love of the outdoors eventually led to her true passion, woodburning. She believes getting outside is good for the soul and seeks most of her inspiration from nature.

As a military wife and stay at home mom, Dana runs her online shop, Elysian Woods, creating original and customized wood-burned art. Since starting her business in 2017, she has been featured on Etsy and in the international RAW Artists tour in Cleveland, Ohio. Day to day, Dana can be found playing with her daughter, drinking too much coffee and eventually burning while the baby sleeps. She feels incredibly blessed to be living her dream making art while inspiring others along the way. Watch Dana's process videos and follow along on her artistic journey on her Instagram page, @ElysianWoods.

GETTING TO KNOW DANA

What was your first woodburning project?

For my first project, I bought some scrap wood squares and burned mandala designs on them.

As a military spouse, how many different places have you lived? Favorite?

Luckily, we've only had to move once, to Georgia. It was a big change from our home of Ohio, and we had tons of fun exploring the south. Georgia will always have a special place in my heart because my daughter was born there!

What's the ideal day?

My ideal day would be waking up to the smell of coffee, going on a little adventure with my family, and maybe a stop at the craft store for some wood shopping! I'd end the day with a glass of wine, good tunes and woodburning.

Are you a maker of other crafts?

As time will allow, yes! My business and family keep me pretty busy. I would love to try macramé next!

What's your favorite ice cream flavor?

Chocolate chip cookie dough

What's your favorite color?

I love teal!

Did you craft as a kid?

I took just about every art class I could throughout my school years!

Do you come from a crafty family?

I grew up helping my dad with his small woodworking projects, mostly birdhouses and lawn decorations. He left some projects unfinished when he passed in 2015. I was lucky enough to be able to repurpose the wood and use it for a few woodburning projects!

When you are inspired by the beauty you find in nature, how do you translate that inspiration to woodburning?

When I get inspired with a new idea to burn, especially nature or animals, I research that subject. I look at tons of pictures online and learn as much as I can, then do my best to capture their beauty through my woodburning art.

Do you have an Instagram creative crush?

Gosh, I feel like I couldn't pick just one. There are SO many talented creatives on Instagram!

Describe your style in one sentence.

Earthy and natural with a touch of boho.

Favorite guilty pleasure?

Crime TV shows. "Law & Order: Special Victims Unit" is my favorite!

What's one thing most people don't know about you?

When I was 16, I traveled to Germany for the summer with two of my best friends.

What advice would you give your daughter as she grows up?

Find your "people." Surround yourself with those who will bring out your best self and cheer you on in life. Find your "thing." Whether it's art, writing, music... it's so very important to create! Lastly, always be authentic and do good for the world.

Do you craft with your daughter?

Absolutely! She is a bit young for most crafts, but she has an art easel next to my desk. Finger painting is a hit right now.

Have any specific artists inspired your work?

I wouldn't say any one specifically, but I would say artists in general inspire me. Before I started selling my art, I always admired other artists on Instagram for pursuing their dreams. It's so beautiful to me how unique every artist is—from their medium to their style.

What advice would you give beginning woodburners?

This craft takes a lot of patience and practice—don't be discouraged by your first few times trying! Find your style and discover what you love to burn.

Do you have a favorite wood you like to burn?

Basswood or birch all the way!

WOODBURNING BASICS

TOOLS

A **woodburning tool kit** with variable temperature control will include everything you need to begin woodburning. The kits are relatively inexpensive and most kits include a variety of points (the small metal tips that screw into the tool end) to use for different techniques and end results. A tool with temperature control allows you to choose which temperature is best for your project.

Although there are many different types of **wood** available for crafting, there are a few variables to keep in mind when choosing a type for woodburning. Light-colored, soft woods with minimal grain are perfect for this art. They allow the tool to glide smoothly on the surface, creating a beautiful contrast between the wood and the burned design. Some favorites include basswood and birch, which are easily found at any craft store.

Graphite transfer paper is the easiest way to transfer designs to wood. Simply trace the design from the book onto tracing paper and tape it where desired on the wood. Place the graphite paper in between, black side down; then use a pen or pencil to draw over the design on the tracing paper.

Sandpaper and **sand erasers** are essentials for woodburning. Use a very fine grit sandpaper to clean residue from your metal points. Sandpaper can also be used to prepare the wood, ensuring a totally smooth surface before burning. While regular erasers can leave a residue, sand erasers are great for fixing small mistakes and cleaning any pencil or graphite paper marks off the wood.

- Stamping Point
- Tapered Point
- Shading Point
- Flow Point
- Universal Point
- Stamping Point
- Mini Flow Point

There are many ways to finish woodburned projects. It's not always necessary to use a stain or sealer, but the piece will be protected and have a more completed look.

- Clear gloss spray **sealer** will protect the design, especially if color was used.

- Light-colored **wood stains** add depth and bring out the beautiful wood grain.

- Cutting boards and kitchen utensils should be sealed with a **food-safe oil**. Cutting board oil is readily available in most stores, but coconut or beeswax oil are great natural options. These wood items should be protected with oil on a regular basis.

BURNING POINTS

While there are many other points that come with your woodburning kit, these 4 will be the most used. Some others include the tapered point, as well as stamping points. My best advice is take some time to get comfortable with the tool and experiment with each point. Dedicate a piece of scrap wood for trying different techiques and learn what works best for you!

UNIVERSAL POINT

The universal point is the most important point to master because it performs many techniques. Use it to burn straight and curved lines by holding it upright and flat against the wood. Lay the point on its side and gently glide across the wood while lifting the point to achieve shading and add depth.

MINI FLOW POINT & FLOW POINT

The mini flow point and flow point are perfect for outlining designs, burning text and adding fine details.

SHADING POINT

The shading point works well for shading large areas and burning leaf or petal designs.

13

IN THE KNOW

One of my most frequently asked questions is how to burn smooth, straight lines. If you are having trouble achieving straight lines, try turning up the heat and using lighter pressure. You should never force the woodburning tool; always allow the heat to do the work.

The points can pick up wood residue as you burn. Remove it by lightly sanding with fine grit sandpaper.

Hold the tool like you would hold a large pencil. You'll get the smoothest lines and burns if you rest your hand on something stable.

Always use spray sealer in a well-ventilated area, preferably outdoors.

Shading is the most difficult technique to master in pyrography. It requires more patience and control than most techniques, but the result is amazing! Shading adds depth and will make the artwork pop, and there are three ways to achieve it with just your universal point.

- Stippling is one of my favorite techniques to burn. Start by burning a thick area of dots in the wood, then taper the dots off slowly and evenly in one direction.

- To achieve classic shading, set your woodburning tool to medium heat. Both temperature and control are very important here. Lay the universal point on its side and glide across the wood, pressing harder at first, then gently lifting to achieve even shading.

- Linework is another fun way to shade. Strart by burning lines close together, then start adding more space between the lines.

SAFETY

While woodburning is a fun hobby, it comes with safety hazards so precautions need to be taken. These tools can reach temperatures of 1000 degrees! Your workspace should be set up on a hard surface, clear of everything, especially fabrics. It's a good idea to tape the included tool stand to your desk. Pets and small children should be kept away from the workspace, and the tool should be turned off and unplugged when not in use.

To change points, turn the woodburning tool off. Allow the point to cool down **completely** before changing to another. Use a small pair of pliers to unscrew and replace points. Changing points while they are hot can break the woodburning tool and ruin the points.

Wearing a mask or using a small desk fan is a great precaution to take while woodburning, especially for those sensitive to fumes. It's very important to only burn on **unfinished** wood. Burning on treated wood releases toxic fumes which are very dangerous to inhale, potentially causing health problems.

BASIC LINEWORK & FILLED AREAS

This project teaches basic linework and filling in designs. Look for an Acacia wood cutting board; this wood is easy to burn & looks beautiful. Avoid bamboo cutting boards, which are much harder to burn because of the wood grain and waxy component of the wood.

Shopping List

- 12" x 16" Acacia wood cutting board
- Woodburning tool with universal point
- Food-safe cutting board oil
- Graphite paper
- Tracing paper

PINEAPPLE CUTTING BOARD

1. This project uses only the universal point. While the woodburning tool is heating up to medium-high heat, trace the design (pattern on page 54) onto tracing paper. Center the design and transfer it onto the cutting board using graphite paper.

18   www.leisurearts.com

2. Burn the outline of the design using the universal point.

3. Adjust the heat to the highest setting. Tilt the tool on its side to fill in the design, turning the tool or cutting board as needed.

4. After burning, wash the cutting board. Seal it using a food-safe oil.

BASIC LETTERING

Learn the basics of lettering while creating a personalized wood slab sign. Lettering can also be used to create a wedding sign, monogram, birth sampler with baby stats or a sports plaque with the player's name and team name.

Shopping List

- Bass wood plaque with bark sides, approximately 5/8" x 8" x 11"
- Woodburning tool with flow point
- Floral embellishments (I used paper flowers)
- Wood sealer (optional)
- Sawtooth hanger
- Graphite paper
- Tracing paper
- Ruler
- Hot glue gun with glue sticks

FAMILY NAME SIGN

1. Trace the desired letter and number combinations (patterns on pages 55-57) onto tracing paper, using a ruler to keep the letters and numbers aligned. Then, transfer the words to the wood using graphite paper. Attach the flow point to the tool and adjust the heat dial to medium-high.

2. Burn the outline of the lettering. To achieve smooth lines, glide the tool gently across the wood in a fluid motion. If needed, adjust the heat to the highest level.

3. Using the same point, begin to fill in the lettering. Use a slow circular motion to achieve a smooth burn.

4. Seal the wood slice after burning if desired. Arrange the flowers on the sign, then glue in place. Attach a sawtooth hanger to the back for easy hanging.

ADDING COLOR

A basic set of watercolors and a small brush are all you need to brighten up a woodburned design. This butterfly is burned entirely with the universal point, clearly indicating that it is very versatile.

Shopping List

- Bass wood plaque with bark sides, about 12" x 8"
- Woodburning tool with universal point
- Yellow and orange watercolor paint
- White acrylic paint
- Clear gloss spray sealer
- (5) 1¼" bronze cup hooks
- Sawtooth hanger
- Small flat paintbrush
- Watercolor dish/palette
- Small cup of water
- Graphite paper
- Tracing paper

BUTTERFLY JEWELRY HANGER

1. Trace the butterfly design (pattern on page 58) onto tracing paper. Center the butterfly design on the wood, then transfer it using graphite paper. Using the universal point on high heat, outline and fill in the design at the same time. Turn the tool and the wood as you work to fill in the spaces.

2. After the design is burned, mix the watercolor paints with water on your dish or palette until the color is thin and transparent. Start by painting the wings yellow, then blend outward changing to orange. Thin coats of paint build up the color and create depth. Let dry.

3. Add the markings to the butterfly with white acrylic paint. After the paint is thoroughly dried, finish the piece with the spray sealer; this will preserve the colors.

4. Make five equally spaced marks on the wood slice under the butterfly. Attach the utility hooks at the marks; then, add a sawtooth hanger to the back for easy hanging.

NATURAL INSPIRATION

I'm constantly inspired by nature's beauty. This watercolored mountain scene is burned on birch, one of my favorite woods, and provides an introduction to capturing natural scenes.

Shopping List

- Birch coaster (3"-4" diameter)
- Woodburning tool with universal point
- Blue watercolor paint
- White acrylic paint
- Clear gloss spray sealer
- 12" length of leather cord
- Small flat paintbrush
- Watercolor dish/palette
- Small cup of water
- Graphite paper
- Tracing paper
- Hand drill

MOUNTAINS ORNAMENT

1. Trace the mountains design (pattern on page 57) onto tracing paper. Center and transfer the design onto the birch coaster. Using the universal point on medium heat, pull the tool gently and evenly to follow the lines without lifting the point from the wood, burning the mountains and tree trunks.

30   www.leisurearts.com

2

3

2. Turn the wood slice to a comfortable position and use quick downward strokes to burn the tree branches.

3. Mix the blue watercolor paint with water on your dish or palette until the color is thin and transparent. Paint the background of the design, using thin coats of paint to build up the color and create depth. Let dry, then use the white acrylic paint to add stars to the sky.

4

4. After the paint is thoroughly dry, finish the ornament with the spray sealer; this will preserve the color. Drill a hole at the ornament top. Loop the leather cord through the ornament hole and knot together near the ends.

ACHIEVING FINE DETAILS

The mini flow point allows you to achieve finer details as you burn the laurel stems and leaves. It may be tricky to find a good place on the tray to rest your hand as you burn. Just keep turning the tray as you work. Then, switch to the univeral point for the lettering.

Shopping List

- 12" x 10" unfinished wood tray
- Woodburning tool with universal point and mini flow point
- Light-colored oil-based wood stain
- Food-safe cutting board oil
- Graphite paper
- Tracing paper

GATHER SERVING TRAY

1. Gently sand the bottom interior of the tray and wipe clean with a damp paper towel. Trace the tray design (pattern on page 59) onto tracing paper. Center the design on the tray and transfer with graphite paper placed between the pattern and tray.

2. Using the universal point on medium high heat, burn the line of the leaf stems. Switch points to the mini flow point for the leaves. This will be tricky without a place to rest your hand. Burn slow and steady on medium heat, turning the tray as you go to find the most comfortable spot to rest your hand while you burn.

3. Outline the lettering using the mini flow point. To fill the letters in, place the universal point on its side and gently drag across the letter using the highest heat setting.

4. Apply one to two coats of stain and allow the tray to air dry. Wash the tray, then allow it to air dry again before applying a food-safe cutting board oil.

ROUNDED SURFACES

Build your woodburning skills (and your patience!) by burning on rounded surfaces like these spoons. The spoon handles are colored with food coloring, making them safe to use in the kitchen.

Shopping List

- Two 12" long unfinished wood spoons
- Woodburning tool with flow point
- Green and blue gel food coloring
- Small flat paintbrush
- Small clear glass bowls to mix food coloring
- Rubbing alcohol
- Food-safe cutting board oil
- Graphite paper
- Tracing paper

SPOONS

1. Trace the spoon designs (patterns on page 60) onto tracing paper. Center the designs on the spoon backs and transfer using graphite paper. Attach the flow point and allow the tool to heat to the medium setting.

2. Begin burning the designs using a steady hand. Go slow and don't rush, burning on a curved surface can be difficult.

3. Burn a line on the handle approximately 3$\frac{5}{8}$" from the end; this will stop the dye from bleeding up the handle. Lay paper down on your work area before dyeing. To make the wood dye, mix approximately 10 drops of food coloring (one color) into $\frac{1}{4}$ cup of rubbing alcohol. Apply two to three coats of the dye. Let dry for at least 24 hours.

4. Burn small designs on the handle if desired. Gently hand wash and coat the spoons with cutting board oil. Spoons should be treated with oil on a regular basis.

SMALLER LETTERING

Don't be afraid to tackle more difficult or smaller lettering, even on a new surface, such as unfinished craft wood. Just go slow and allow the heated burner tool to do the work.

Shopping List

- Set of 3 unfinished wood planters with base (Each planter should be about 4" x 4" x 4").
- Woodburning tool with mini flow point
- Light-colored oil-based wood stain
- Clear gloss spray sealer
- Graphite paper
- Fine grit sandpaper
- Tracing paper
- Succulents

PLANTER SET

1. Gently sand the planters and base; wipe clean with a damp paper towel. Trace the quotes (patterns on page 61) onto tracing paper. Center each quote design on a planter, then transfer using graphite paper. Allow the woodburning tool to heat up to medium heat with the mini flow point attached.

42   www.leisurearts.com

2. Find a comfortable spot to rest your hand on the planter, turning the planter while burning if needed. Slowly burn the outline of the lettering and fill in as you go.

3. After the lettering is burned, apply two coats of stain, allowing stain to dry about 30 minutes between coats. Once stain is completely dry, apply two coats of spray sealer and allow to dry.

4. Fill the planters with different types and sizes of succulents.

USING MULTIPLE POINTS

Birch is a harder wood, but is good for practicing your burning techniques as you use more than one point for these designs. Making these coasters will build your watercoloring skills, as well as your woodburning skills.

Shopping List

- Four 4" diameter birch coasters
- Woodburning tool with universal point and mini flow point
- Green, yellow-green, brown and pink watercolor paints
- Small round paintbrush
- Watercolor dish/palette
- Small cup of water
- Clear gloss spray sealer
- Graphite paper
- Tracing paper

1

SUCCULENT COASTERS

1. Trace the succelent patterns (page 62) onto tracing paper. Transfer the designs to the coasters while the woodburning tool is heating up to the highest setting with the universal point.

46 www.leisurearts.com

2

2. Use the universal point to burn the linework and the mini flow point to finish the smaller details and curves, such as the designs on the planters. Add spines to the Saugaro cactus as desired.

3. Mix the watercolor paints with water on your dish or palette until the color is thin and transparent. Wet a section of the design on the wood coaster with the watercolor brush before adding color. While painting, blend two shades of green for each succulent to add depth. Thin coats of paint build up the color. Paint the planters brown then add a pop of color on the planter's details.

4. After the paint has dried, coat the coasters with spray sealer. To ensure the coasters are waterproof, apply 5-10 coats, letting the sealer dry between each application.

SHADING

This more advanced and intricate mandala uses two techniques for shading, one of the hardest techniques to master. Both stippling and classic shading combine to create depth and interest on the mandala.

Shopping List

- 7" diameter birch round with bark sides
- 6 yards of assorted ½" wide ribbons
- 3 yards of thin twine
- 12" length of leather cord
- 6 wooden beads that can be threaded on ribbon
- 10 metallic gold craft feathers
- Woodburning tool with universal point and mini flow point
- Electric drill with small bit
- Graphite paper
- Tracing paper

MANDALA WALL HANGING

1. While the woodburning tool is heating up to the highest setting, trace the mandala design (pattern on page 63) onto tracing paper. Center and transfer the mandala design onto the birch round using graphite paper.

2. Begin burning the outline of the design using the universal point. All linework should be done with this point.

3. Switch to the mini flow point to complete the more detailed aspects of the design.

4. Add depth to the mandala by shading and stippling a few areas. The universal point makes a great shading tool when used on its side.

5. Drill one hole at the top of the wood slice for hanging. Drill five holes, equally spaced, along the bottom. Thread the jute and desired ribbons through the holes at the bottom and knot close to the wood slice. Attach beads and feathers at the ribbon ends to add texture.

6. Loop the leather cord through the hole at the top and knot the ends together for easy hanging.

PATTERNS

PINEAPPLE

When tracing patterns, only trace the outlines of the shapes; it is not necessary to color in the shape on the tracing.

FAMILY NAME SIGN

55

FAMILY NAME SIGN

FAMILY NAME SIGN

1234567890

ESTABLISHED

MOUNTAINS ORNAMENT

BUTTERFLY JEWELRY HANGER

GATHER SERVING TRAY

SPOONS

SMALL PLANTERS

Bloom with grace

Let your dreams blossom

Grow where you are planted

SUCCELENT COASTERS

MANDALA WALL HANGING

Library of Congress Control Number: 2019933050.

Made in China.

Copyright © 2019 by Leisure Arts, Inc., 104 Champs Blvd., STE 100, Maumelle, AR 72113-6738, www.leisurearts.com. All rights reserved. This publication is protected under federal copyright laws. Reproduction or distribution of this publication or any other Leisure Arts publication, including publications which are out of print, is prohibited unless specifically authorized. This includes, but is not limited to, any form of reproduction or distribution on or through the Internet, including posting, scanning, or e-mail transmission.

We have made every effort to ensure that these instructions are accurate and complete. We cannot, however, be responsible for human error, typographical mistakes, or variations in individual work.

Production Team: Technical Editor – Mary Sullivan Hutcheson; Technical Associate Editor – Lisa Lancaster; Senior Graphic Artist – Lora Puls; Graphic Designer – Kate Moul; Photo Stylist – Lori Wenger; Photographer – Jason Masters.